God Given

An Accounting of
His Unmistakable Blessings

LORI DEVILLEZ

First Edition – 2016

Bluffton, Indiana

First Editor Copyright – 2016
by Lori DeVillez

ISBN 9781628009989

ENDORSEMENTS

It was such an honor to read Lori's book in its pre-published form. Having known Lori from her early assignment at the pregnancy resource center here in Evansville to her current, much expanded role as the Executive Director of APRC, it has been a privilege to watch her life in God unfold in all its many and various facets.

The stories within speak for themselves, but I would like to speak to the person God has used in bringing these stories to life through her obedience and faith. She is the real deal. She walks in such meekness and humility but, much like Jesus, humility does not mean powerless... it just means power under control, so it is spent only on the things of the Kingdom.

From that place of strength and resolve, you will see again and again in these pages, she never backs down from a fight if she knows God has her name on it.

But of all the accomplishments, the changes she has wrought on many levels for LIFE, the miracles she has seen God bring through the work of her hands and heart over and over... in individual lives, in finances, in the courts, in missions, in movements... of all these things you read about in these pages, what I admire most about Lori and actually have a holy jealousy over, is her prayer life. Undoubtedly, the secret weapon in her arsenal.

She walks in intimacy with the Lord in a way available to all, but chosen by few. And I have no doubt, that this book is but a glimpse of the stories written in heaven, of the lives she has impacted, imparted to, or rescued. To God be the glory.

Linda Ramsey, MD, FACOG
Medical Director, Pregnancy Resource Center, Evansville, IN
Senior Board Member, House of Prayer Evansville

God-Given is a reminder of God's faithfulness to His children when they trust Him in ALL things. You will be inspired and challenged to a new level of faith as you read about Lori Devillez's life journey and her quest to advance the culture of life.

Gloria Leyda, Sr. Vice President
Ambassador Speakers Bureau

Some would say that they have never seen God do a miracle. Some would say that He doesn't even do miracles any more. To such people I say "read this book". Lori fills it with the undeniable miracles she has witnessed and often been a part of.

Some would say that they never see prayer answered. To them I say "read this book". Lori shows how fervent prayer for God's will to be done has often been answered in miraculous ways.

I have known Lori for many years. I have witnessed her huge vision and untiring work. I am in awe of her and so glad she has taken the time to share with all of us her testimony to God's goodness and faithfulness. She encourages us all in these pages.

Joe McIlhaney, M.D., Founder/Chairman
The Medical Institute for Sexual Health

During years of hosting radio and television talk shows, I've *Love Walked* with thousands of authors, ministry leaders, pastors and ordinary people. Most of them were powerful men and women, but few are like Lori DeVillez who is a "Life Saver." Lori's love for Jesus and others, births life for the unborn, and new life and love for both moms and dads.

Evelyn W. Davison— Love Talk Network, The Good News Journal, Inc., NDP-CTTF, and Author: *"Praying and Praising Across Texas."*

Do not read this book unless you're ready to be gripped, challenged and reminded of God's power to accomplish His mighty work through ordinary people like Lori – and you! This refreshing account of God's life-giving work through the gospel of Christ crucified will draw you heavenward, even as it firmly plants your feet in the here-and-now, preparing you to walk in the good works God has prepared for your brief pilgrimage.

Jay Hobbs
Heartbeat International
Director of Marketing and Communication

A book written about what God can and will do through a willing and obedient heart is best told by someone who lives this in their life and ministry. Those of us who know Lori, know this book is an overflow of her life and experience. She lives this abundant life that God promises! Be encouraged, God is still doing great things.

Dr. David W. Smith
Executive Director, Austin Baptist Association

DEDICATION

It is my great privilege to dedicate this book to my parents, Pat and Wayne DeVillez. It is through their love and sacrifice that I have learned to seek the Lord Jesus in all of my endeavors.

FOREWORD

I have been gifted with a ringside seat, and the ability to actually watch the miracles unfold, as God blesses Lori DeVillez and the people He has purposed her to love and help.

I promise you, there is no true end to this book. Since Lori finished her manuscript, the miracles of God's provision have continued to happen with astounding regularity. I believe that is because our Savior knows from experience He can trust Lori with His divine gifts, whether they be material to pass on, or financial to help those in need. Lori is always available to serve her Lord.

The day I "got" how much Jesus loves His servant Lori DeVillez, we were delivering a load of donated items to James Bruner TK Ranch, a home for special needs adults where my niece Elizabeth lives. Lori had rented a big box-truck, filled it to the max, and driven it the 220 miles from Austin to the ranch in Sunset, Texas.

TK Ranch is out in the country where the roads are unpaved, but they have a road-base of caliche, a combination of gravel and sand that creates an incredible amount of dust. The dust got so thick on the truck's windshield we couldn't see, and when Lori tried to get it off with the washer and windshield wipers, no water came out! At that exact moment a rain shower lasting a matter of seconds fell from the cloudless sky, the wipers cleared the dust, and we could see the road again. It was amazingly convenient and we laughed at our good fortune.

We unloaded the truck and headed back down the caliche road. Shortly, the windshield was completely covered with dust and visibility was down to zero. Lori turned on the wipers, hoping to at least knock off some of the dust, and another short burst of rain fell from the clear skies and rinsed the windshield clean. This time we both knew it hadn't been a coincidence when it happened earlier, and I marveled at how specifically God was taking care of His girl Lori. We laughed and rejoiced at how intimate our Lord is, how much He is into the details, and how no need is too small or too great for Him to fill.

As we turned onto the paved farm-to-market road, God blessed us with one more short burst of rain from the still cloudless sky and we were able to see clearly all the way home.

It is my prayer as you read Lori's accolades for the One she loves most, that you, too, will see more clearly God's loving hand in your life and marvel at the extent of His love for you.

Because He lives...
Joshua 1:9

Julie Ziglar Norman

INTRODUCTION

Thank you for taking the time to pick up this book. We are embarking on a journey together that will astonish you. At times, I am sure, you will scratch your head and ask, "How could that be?" It is my prayer that this book will not only inspire you, but will also bring you hope and encouragement that as you serve God you will experience "GOD-GIVEN" blessings, just as I have.

Have you ever asked the questions:

Why am I here?

What is my purpose in life?

Is there more to life than just eating, sleeping and going to work?

Is there such a thing as having your steps ordered or having a specific assignment in life?

These are some of the questions I've asked myself many times and they are one of the reasons I've decided to sit down and write to you today. I have experienced exciting, awe-inspiring things that defy explanation, and they are too miraculous to keep to myself. Have you ever had that happen to you, when something was so amazing you exclaimed, "Wow!" and then gave yourself the quiz – "How did that happen? Why did that happen? How could that have happened?"

There have also been many times when I did not understand why I was having to do certain things, and prayed to God that I could be relieved from them or released to do something else. However, as I stayed obedient to God and continued to trust Him, I learned that He is always faithful to see me through to the other side. So many of the things that I learned during difficult times are being used for the assignment I have today. I am forever grateful that He truly does order our steps if we will but trust Him.

BRING THEM UP IN THE WAY THEY SHOULD GO

Some would consider it miraculous that I came to know Jesus as Lord and Savior at a very early age. I regularly attended a Good News Backyard Club in my neighborhood and it was there that I asked Jesus into my life. I applaud all children's ministry workers. There are philosophies that young children do not really understand enough to make a decision, but I can attest to the fact that I understood at the age of six. I understood that I was not perfect and made mistakes, and that I needed some way to find forgiveness. Jesus came to live a perfect life on earth, and made a way through His sacrifice for me to find that forgiveness.

I am grateful for Child Evangelism Fellowship workers and the enduring friendship of Herman and Doris Bass and their faithfulness to follow His call for their lives. It was in their backyard that I came to know Jesus! It has been one breathtaking journey ever since. He is the foundation of the life I've lived. As the Scriptures tell us - *we shall know the truth and the truth will set us free.* With His forgiveness and freedom, we can live the abundant life right here on earth!

At the age of nine, I knew beyond a shadow of a doubt that I wanted to be a missionary. In my childish mind, a missionary was simply someone who goes to live in a foreign country to share the love of Jesus. So, I began searching for the country I was supposed to go to.

My family attended a small Baptist church as I was growing up, and I loved being part of the youth group. In fact, my first leadership position came about when I became president of the youth group by the end of my freshman year in high school. The wonderful memories of the ministry activities and the fun things we did as a group still make me smile.

I have been very blessed all my life to have great mentors. I know I bragged on my parents in my tribute to them, but I want you to know that I consider them my mentors, as well. They always encouraged me to follow my heart and deepen my love for Jesus. In middle school I was also blessed with a wonderful Sunday school teacher, Becky Armitage, who took me under her wing. She called me every day after school to find out how my day went, and if I was able to share Jesus with anyone. She also challenged me weekly with my Scripture memorization and gave me wonderful advice about friendships; to have great friends and enjoy their fellowship, but to remember that Jesus is my very best friend, always!

By the time I was a junior in high school I began searching for more. I wanted to travel to different countries in hopes of finding the country I would eventually serve as a missionary. When I received a flyer in the mail inviting me to "Visit the Open Door," a youth group at a much larger church in Evansville, I invited a friend and we went together. It was FANTASTIC! The youth pastor, David Schwambach, was extraordinary and immediately took me under his wing to help me identify my gifts and talents and how I could use them in the youth group.

My first official title was: "Pass-Out Minister." Pastor Dave would have me passing out flyers and handouts. Then I got involved in the "Helps" ministries. That means I helped everywhere they needed help: ushering, greeting, preparing for events, etc. It was a fun, growing experience.

To this very day, 35 years later, Pastor Dave Schwambach is still a remarkable mentor to me. I am grateful to have had the leadership of a man who looks only to Jesus and follows His example. I have never known a pastor to give and do so very much, all from his heart of love for Jesus and His sheep. I thank God for Pastor Dave, and for the legacy he has given me.

OFF TO THE MISSION FIELD

After I graduated from high school and completed one year of college, I signed up to go on a mission trip to Durango City, in Durango, Mexico, with six people from my new church. I learned so much from that trip. First there was the matter of fundraising, and preparing spiritually and emotionally to be all that God wanted me to be as I served those in ministry to Him. I felt ready when we arrived, and began serving through the Bible School and also through manual labor in clearing grounds for a sports field and helping build a church. Looking back, I can see that even the preparation for the long drive and the three weeks we served taught me skills I still use today.

Before going on the trip to Mexico, our church had acquired an old monastery that they wanted to make into a community outreach. Part of that outreach would be a benevolence program, hot meal program, clothing program, pregnancy center, and a maternity home. I remember meeting Mary Jo Pea, who ultimately led our trip to Mexico, in the abandoned house of the monastery. There was no electricity at the time and it was cold, but we met from 6:00 a.m. to 7:00 a.m. every Tuesday morning for prayer. Little did I know that I would get to help start the ministries and then one day be the director of two of them.

On our drive back from Mexico we stopped at International Bible College in San Antonio, Texas. Our trip leader, Mary Jo, had graduated from IBC and I enjoyed learning about the different classes they offered and meeting the people she introduced me to. I also learned that Mary Jo, who was single at the time, was planning to go to Japan to serve as a career missionary, but needed someone to travel with her to raise her financial support. I immediately said that I could take a year off from college and travel with her.

When we got home I talked with my parents about taking the year off from school. I have always sought my parents' blessing in all of my endeavors. I believe this is honoring to God and brings blessing upon my life, and it blesses them. They gave their blessing on one condition, that after the year of travel I would return and complete my Bachelor's degree at the university. I quickly agreed!

That year on the road was totally amazing. I studied the different churches that we would visit and the pastoral leadership all across the country. I met so many people, and learned how to present a ministry for people to invest in. It was a dedicated time of learning and growing and being challenged.

After the year of travel, I decided to sign up to go to International Bible College in San Antonio for a semester. It was during that semester that I connected with some students from Japan. I learned as much as I could about their language, their culture, and a great deal about their food, etc. Primarily, I learned that the Japanese are an uncommon people.

When the semester was over I went home to keep the promise I had made to my parents. I re-entered the University of Southern Indiana to complete my degree with a double major in psychology/social work and with a minor in Spanish. I made great friends with many of the students and the professors, and I had the awesome opportunity to complete an internship with autistic children funded by the Sylvester Stallone Foundation. I traveled to various schools and facilities for autistic students, and our team collected data and wrote a book to support the thought that autism is genetic rather than environmental. It was a great study.

All the while, I was studying many things under Pastor Dave Schwambach's mentorship. We had developed a strong team for the Junior High Ministry and I had become one of the key leaders. We took mission trips to Crandon, Wisconsin, on the Indian reservations and even stayed at Moody Bible Institute with the students. I had so much fun being on a bowling team with some of the junior high leaders. Even now, we still celebrate our strong bond and the blessing of the special memories that we share.

Never one to rest on my laurels, I also signed up and completed a semester of Evangelism Explosion under Pastor Dave's leadership. Evangelism Explosion is a 16-week semester course for learning the Scriptures for evangelism and then going out and applying them. We spent an hour in the classroom each week with a mentor and our accountability partner, then we would go out into the community, to places like people's homes, malls, hospitals, and nursing homes to apply what we had learned. I, yet today, train this amazing tool in evangelism with the pregnancy resource centers all across the country.

Upon graduation with my Bachelor of Arts in Psychology and Social Work, I traveled and spent the summer as a short-term missionary to Japan. I worked the first month in the Language Institute for Evangelism (LIFE) offices. It was really cool, learning how to take the trains to and from the office and to go shopping on my own.

The second month I served a church in Okinawa, and the last month we traveled back up to Tokyo by way of Osaka. I loved meeting the people, learning the culture, and serving in various capacities. I was even asked to sing English songs at a Japanese wedding; however, I was very glad when it was time to head back home to the United States.

My adventures had taught me that I was not called to Mexico, nor was I called to Japan. So my question remained, "Where am I to serve as a missionary?"

Shortly after I returned from Japan, I was contacted by the professor at the University of Southern Indiana that I had studied with on the autism project. She wanted to know if I would be interested in working as her assistant in the newly-created Graduate Studies Department. I was very excited to have employment; however, I knew I was still in search of my mission. "Lord, I'll take this job You have put before me, but I remain ready to serve. Show me where You want me to go."

It was fun to be part of the beginning of something new while working in the Graduate Studies Department, and I learned many things God needed for me to know. Learning the administrative processes needed to begin a new department has served me well, as have the things I learned about graduate business management, people communication skills, and what I learned from the graduate psychology counseling courses I was able to take for free as an employee of the university. I believe my ability to pioneer many new things along my journey is largely a result of this experience.

After working at the university for two years I was given an opportunity to help with the development of a licensed daycare center that was being opened by a local hospital. One of the professors that I had met at the university was heading up the project, and wanted to see if I'd be interested in helping her get the new daycare off of the ground. I thought it sounded like a great opportunity, so I began working with the hospital. This was, once again, another opportunity to pioneer something that had not been done before in Evansville. It was there that I met many doctors and healthcare professionals. After the daycare was up and running I transferred to the administration offices of the hospital.

THE VOLUNTEER

At about the time I started working with the hospital, Pastor David and Judy Merwin returned to Evansville after serving in South Korea for nearly 20 years. I began spending time with them to learn more about the life of a missionary. They, along with their two remarkable daughters that they adopted from Korea, Stephanie and Sarah, quickly took me in as part of their family. It was great fun for me to listen to all of them and learn how to be bold in sharing Jesus everywhere you go. I also learned how Pastor Merwin multiplied churches while in South Korea. It would be years later when God would move me to Austin, Texas, that I would apply what I learned from him.

At about this time, my church had begun a new series challenging people to learn what their God-ordained spiritual gifts are and live them out in a practical way by serving. I participated in what the church was doing, and discovered that my highest spiritual gifts were evangelism, administration, and helps. We were encouraged to sign up for ministries that matched our gifts, so I volunteered for just about everything, including youth ministry, office work, and a pregnancy resource center.

After working in the hospital's administration department, I accepted a job offer from Dr. Morrison, an OB/GYN doctor I met at the hospital when I was taking graduate courses. Initially, I didn't understand why I was working at the OB/GYN office, because I did not enjoy ANYTHING medical. I dreaded being called into the patient's room to assist the doctor with exams. I certainly did not enjoy it when the doctor, in an enthusiastic effort to educate me, would insist on showing me sexually transmitted diseases under the microscope. Thankfully, God eventually gave me the following insight so that I could fully take advantage of the opportunity He had given me.

If you will recall, one of the places I volunteered to serve after I learned what my gifts were, was at the pregnancy resource center. On the day I received my first call from the director of the pregnancy center, she announced that she was going out of town that weekend and needed to bring me the key so I could open the center. I had never been to the center, because by that time they had moved the center out of the monastery, and I had not had any training, formal or otherwise, as to what they did there. I had only signed up to volunteer. I shared with her that I might not be the best person to leave the key with. She explained that there would be another trained volunteer there, so I would not be alone. My thought was, "Then let them have the key!" That was probably not the nicest thought to have, but I'll be honest with you - that was my first thought.

I agreed to go open the center that Saturday, and when I arrived, there was a girl sitting and waiting at the top of the stairs leading up to the front door. I asked if she was the volunteer for the day and she replied, "No, I'm here for a pregnancy test."

My heart began to race. I began thinking, "Now what do I do?" I had never done a pregnancy test in my life! However, with my formal training in psychology/social work, I had learned to never let them see you sweat, stay calm, and move on with confidence. So I said, "No problem, come on in. I can help!" All the while knowing I had no idea what I was doing!

Fortunately, I was able to follow instructions to run the pregnancy test, and her test results were negative. We ended up having a great conversation and when I shared the Good News of Jesus, she prayed to receive Him into her heart that day!

I got so excited! I went back to work that following Monday and I finally KNEW what my mission was! I wanted to learn all about pregnancy and OB care and sexually transmitted diseases, because I saw how all of those things could impact a life. I realized that by serving those who were in crisis and afraid they might be pregnant, I could help them and share Jesus at the same time! I loved every part of the mission! God had me in "on-the-job training" with the OB/GYN office all the time. I had found my assignment!

BECOMING DIRECTOR

I had been volunteering at the pregnancy resource center for four years when the director of the center gave her resignation. I loved volunteering, and I had gotten to know a lot of the people with the Life Center, so I looked forward to my time there.

After the director's resignation, the Executive Director of the Evansville Christian Life Center called and asked to meet with me. I thought I knew what she wanted. As I prayed about the meeting, I laid out a plan of what I knew I would need to be paid in order to leave the OB/GYN office to work full-time at the Life Center.

Amazingly, when I went to the meeting the Executive Director let me know that they were interested in hiring me to direct BOTH the pregnancy resource center and the maternity home. She laid out a plan for me and it was exactly everything that I had laid out in my prayer time! It is astounding how clear God makes our path as we wholeheartedly seek Him!

THE FOUNTAIN

When I became the director for the pregnancy resource center and maternity home, I wanted to make changes to make us more efficient. At the time, we did not have any computers at either location.

One day I was walking at the mall and praying about how to get a computer to manage our data and be more effective with our time. As I was walking past the fountain in the mall, my attention was drawn to the coins in the fountain. Then I got creative. "What if we could receive the coins from the fountain for one month and raise enough funds to purchase a computer for the pregnancy resource center?" Because I have always lived by "we have not because we ask not," I decided to go to the mall management and ask if they would consider my idea. The manager said, "Yes!"

I researched how much money I would need to purchase a computer and came to the conclusion that I would need about $700. I stand amazed that at the end of that month the amount that came in from the coins from the fountain was exactly $700! Our God supplies all of our needs in the most excellent way!

THE DOUBLE OVEN

The maternity home I was managing could house up to five pregnant girls at a time. One of the messages we always taught our girls was that God will supply all of our needs and He does it with excellence. However, I was concerned that what we were saying and what the girls actually saw, sent two different messages because the home was not in the best shape. I went to my supervisor and asked, "If I could get the funding, would it be okay to make improvements to the home?" She gave her approval, so I went in search of funding.

Within just a few months we were approved for a $17,000 grant. This was very exciting to me. However, I knew that I would need additional resources to do a complete home makeover.

I developed a plan for each room and specifics of what I would want to change and upgrade to make the home warm and inviting and in the most excellent condition. In the writing of the grant, I had only allocated $1,500 for the remodel of the kitchen. I knew I would need much more than that to accomplish a whole new kitchen.

I went to several of the home improvement stores in town and asked to speak to the managers about my project. Everywhere I went, everyone was excited about what I was doing and they were willing to help. Because it was near the end of the year, one place offered to donate top-of-the-line cabinets, a range top, a new sink and fixtures. The only appliance that they did not have was a double oven. Our project manager had already cut the hole for the double oven, so we knew the size and place where it would go.

As I was driving back to the Life Center that day, I was excited and had so much gratitude for all that we had been given, but I was asking the Lord what we would do for the double oven. Where would it come from? When I arrived back at my office, sitting right there on the porch was a double oven! It wasn't even in a box. I was so excited! I was amazed! I was in awe!

I went into my supervisor's office and asked her if she knew anything about the double oven on the porch? She said that she did not. I called our project engineer and asked him if the double oven would work in our kitchen. He came to look at it. He, too, was in awe!

He said it was the perfect fit, the exact same color as the other appliances, and that it was a brand new oven! To this day, I do not know when or how the double oven came to be on the porch of the Life Center, but this I know, God provides for all of our needs according to His riches in glory!

TOUCH OF CLASS

As we were performing the makeover on the maternity home, we decided we wanted to change the colors from the faded pink carpet to a nice, plush teal with specks of purple. It was beautiful carpet that added warmth and elegance to the home. We put the carpet throughout the home on all three floors and even found a new couch and chair that perfectly matched.

We gave the tired-looking walls a nice fresh coat of paint and cleaned and reorganized most of the furniture. We were nearly finished with the home makeover when I received a call from a store called *Touch of Class* saying that they had end-of-line inventory they would like to donate to us. I was excited to receive the inventory, but what I didn't know is that God was putting the finishing touches on our home makeover to bless the girls who came to live with us.

When the inventory arrived it included wallpaper to add another touch of class to our freshly-painted walls, and the wallpaper was a perfect match: purple and teal! We also received miniature lamps that were teal with the shades a wonderfully balanced purple and teal.

Our new home was filled with the warmth of everything matching and flowing together, and we were able to complete the makeover with the added touch of class for the original grant of $17,000! Truly a miracle of how God provides in His most excellent way!

A BRAND NEW MINI-VAN

The maternity home van was in a horribly rundown condition. It was so bad that you could see the street through the hole in the floor. Our teaching that God provides and He does it with excellence was in question where the girls were concerned, so once again I went to my supervisor and asked if I could raise the money or find a resource for another vehicle would it be ok. After much discussion I was given approval.

We began contacting car lots and requesting the donation of new vans so we could drive our girls to their appointments, school, church, etc. One day we were contacted by a husband and wife who owned one of the car lots in town. They said they were interested in learning more about us.

We were thrilled to have them tour our facility. After a very pleasant visit, the wife shared that they wanted to donate a van because at one point in her life, she had been in a very similar situation as the girls. They approved us for a brand new mini-van.

I'll never forget the day we went to pick it up. When we drove it off the lot the odometer registered only 15 miles. It was perfect! Once again, God provided for our need in the most excellent way!

THE LEFT SHOES

While working for the Life Center we never knew what kind of donations would come in each day – we accepted far more than just money. When donations did come in, we immediately prayed about where they were to go.

One day we received a shipment of brand new shoes; however, they were a size 5 and only for the left foot! What were we to do with these?

What do you know? We had a lady come in for assistance whose right leg had been amputated. She was looking for a size 5 shoe for her left foot. She said she had prayed that we would have the size she needed and that she only needed the shoes for that one foot. Amazing how God provides for the specifics! She was blessed and so were we!

ENLARGING THE TERRITORY

After directing the pregnancy resource center and maternity home for four years in my hometown, an opportunity came for me to work with pregnancy resource centers on a statewide basis in Texas. However, I was involved in a lot of different endeavors and wanted to make sure that this was the move I was to make. I decided to take two weeks to fast and pray before accepting the position in Texas.

During that two weeks, when I passed people in the hall at the Life Center they would ask me when I was moving to Texas. I had told no one about the opportunity. I asked them why they would ask that and every single person said the same thing, "God's got a big plan!"

I decided to talk with my parents and get their blessing. I talked with my dad first, and let him know that while I was visiting in Texas I was offered a position that would network pregnancy resource centers throughout the State of Texas. He said that when I went to visit, that he and mom had prayed and they knew I would be offered a position. However, he said I would need to talk with my mom.

When I talked with my mom she agreed and said, "Your time here is done, it is time for you to go." I accepted the opportunity to move to Texas, and every responsibility I had in my hometown was already provided for as people who were working with me stepped up to cover the work that needed to be done. I was amazed at how smooth the transition was.

My life has been a very exciting adventure ever since I made the move to Texas! There is no better place to be than in the middle of God's specific plan for you.

Hannah Nicole DeVillez

In the year 2000, our family was blessed with my one and only and most favorite niece in the whole wide world. All new life is a miracle, and I find it fascinating when a new generation comes into being. There is such freshness and excitement about the potential of that little life and all the adventures that lie ahead!

I knew right away that I wanted Hannah to know her "Aunt Lo," and that I wanted to be very involved in her life. I made a strategic plan to see her in every quarter of the year in her early life so she would know me and what I do. But even more than that, I wanted to know her and the special gifts that God had created within her. I wanted to have influence in her life in hopes that she would always seek God, put Him first, and fulfill her God-ordained destiny!

We began taking adventure trips when Hannah turned two years of age. It is especially fun spending time together now that she is sixteen years old. I love it when we talk about our memories of the trips we have taken. Together we retraced the founding fathers' steps in the Northeast, visited New York City, and Disney World in Florida, travelled to Los Angeles and Santa Monica, California (feeding ducks), as well as the beach in Alabama, and all of her trips to Texas in between.

Every time she comes to Texas I give her a new responsibility at the Austin Pregnancy Resource Center. When she was little she would clean the babies and learn about how they grow and develop. When she grew older she began to observe sonograms, and she has since learned how to greet the clients at the reception desk and serve them in the boutique.

She is becoming a very special and wise young lady and I know she will stay focused and on-target for the plans God has for her life. She has my commitment that I will stand with her in helping her reach God's purposes for her life. I am very proud of her!

PRAYER FOR A NEW PREGNANCY RESOURCE CENTER

Upon moving to Texas my first question was: "Where is the pregnancy resource center near the University of Texas campus?" There are 50,000 students enrolled at UT and 20,000 international students. There were four abortion facilities at the time surrounding the campus and not a single pregnancy resource center.

Let me ask you a question: "Have you ever had a dream deep in your heart that you knew needed to happen, but everyone in your world told you why it would never happen?" I had a dream for a new pregnancy resource center to be located at the UT campus, but everyone told me why it would never happen: UT is the number one "party school"; it is the most expensive property in Austin; you will never get volunteers to come to downtown Austin, and on and on.

I stopped talking to people and took it to God. I knew He had planted the vision in my heart. A friend of mine started going with me to pray over the campus and the State Capitol every Monday from 12:00-12:30. We were asking God to raise up godly leadership for our state, to change the laws in our state, and to raise up a pregnancy resource center at the UT campus. There had been no pro-life laws passed in the State of Texas since 1985. After we started praying at the Capitol, three pro-life bills passed in the next legislative session! The National Abortion Rights Action League (NARAL) grades every state according to access to abortion and, at that time, Texas was at an A-minus. I'm here to report to you today that Texas is now graded at an F! Prayer works! Today, Texas leads the nation in the most effective pro-life laws on the books!

After seven years of going downtown to pray, God decided it was time for the Austin Pregnancy Resource Center to open. A couple of new pastors had come to Austin and one of them was the new pastor at the church I was attending. I went to meet Pastor Michael Lewis, and shared my vision and what I do. Instead of telling me why a new pregnancy resource center by UT would never happen, he asked me what it would cost to make it happen. I shared with him that it would cost around $200,000. He said, "Let's do it!" He joined with another new pastor to Austin, Ryan Rush, and between the two of them they raised the funds to cover the first three years of financing for the center!

We held our first organizational meeting in October 2004 and 91 people attended. We put a plan together and set an opening date for January 16, 2005. After seven years of praying and within 52 days (we call it the building of the Nehemiah wall), the Austin Pregnancy Resource Center came into being. We had 500 people attend our grand opening day!

The vision of the Austin Pregnancy Resource Center is to Build a Culture of Life by being a model center to duplicate itself anywhere in the world.

THE MOVING TRUCK

I apologized to my dog Ari as she eyed the small space she had to snuggle into for us to make our way from Austin, Texas, to Evansville, Indiana, for my traditional family Christmas. As usual, I had packed the car to the hilt with presents and ministry resources to bless the folks at home. The bottom layer of blessings was case upon case of Bibles to give to my friend, Pastor Steve Schwambach, who had just started a new church.

My mom went with me to take the Bibles to Pastor Steve, and I was sharing with her how badly our ministry needed a moving truck. God's blessings had given us so many resources that I needed a moving truck to handle them all! As we turned the corner into the parking lot of Pastor Steve's church, there sat a moving truck with a big "For Sale" sign! I asked Pastor Steve about the truck but he didn't have any information. I called the number on the sign and was delighted to discover that the truck belonged to a friend of mine! I had taught his daughter in her junior high youth group.

I had a great time visiting with Joe Kastle that day, and I shared my vision for the truck. He met me at the church so I could take the 16-foot box truck for a test drive. I was already excited that it had an automatic transmission, but I got super-excited when I learned that he was selling it for $3,500! I knew I would be driving that truck back to Texas!

I took pictures of the truck and posted them on Facebook along with my vision for the truck and why the ministry needed it so badly. Before I left Evansville, the moving truck was paid for! My mom and sister-in-law blessed me by following me back to Texas in my car.

God keeps the truck full and we continue to distribute all of the amazing blessings He bestows on us.

HAS THERE BEEN OPPOSITION?

I must pause here and share with you that during the first two years of opening the Austin Pregnancy Resource Center there was intense battle. I honestly did not know what to do. There was warfare everywhere.

One Sunday night at church I was crying out to God, asking Him what to do. I was led to go forward to the altar and talk with one of the pastors who actually served as music minister at the time. I thought that was strange, but I was desperate!

I shared with him that I needed to talk with him. He encouraged me to call his office the next day and make an appointment. I was able to get in the next day. (I learned later that people often wait months to get in to see him.) When I sat down across from his desk, he asked how he could help me. I answered, "I honestly don't know." I said, "I don't know why I'm sitting in a music minister's office and I know nothing about music!"

He laughed and shared with me that he was the spiritual warfare counselor for the church. Wow! God had led me again to the perfect place and person!

He asked me if I knew that I was where God wanted me to be. I shared with him that I truly didn't know, because Indiana was looking really good to me about then. He told me to go home and pray and get in the Word and come back in a week. He said, "I think I know what you need to do, but I want God to tell you."

I did what he said and it was clear I was where I needed to be. I told him that when I returned for my appointment the next week. He said, "Then put your hand to the plow and move forward.

Don't look back!" That was some of the most powerful advice he could have given me. We continue to move forward!

FINDING THE PERFECT FACILITY

When we began the process of planning to open the Austin Pregnancy Resource Center we knew the location of our facility would be key. Some people told us to go East of IH 35 in Austin, but I knew that we would need to be in the heart of where the students are. We had $3,500 a month allocated in the new budget for the facility.

Our realtor pulled a list of locations and we began going out and looking. Nothing matched what we could afford in the location we desired. After we had exhausted all of the possibilities on our list, we were driving down Rio Grande Street when we saw a two-story house with a For Lease sign on the corner of the lot. The location was not on our original list.

We called and asked if we could see the house and it was a perfect fit. We negotiated with the building owner and he agreed to work within our budget! Little did we know that the facility is located in the West Campus of the University of Texas, the exact location where the students live. We are smack dab in the center of sororities and fraternities and condos and apartments. The area known at UT for student housing. It is absolutely perfect!

FORMULA?

The Austin Pregnancy Resource Center had not been open very long when we received a call from a young mom in need, who asked if we had any baby formula. She explained that her baby was a week old and had only had water for the past two days. I asked her to come to the center and told her we would help her. At that time, we didn't have any formula, but I gathered our volunteers together and we stopped and prayed and asked God to provide for this young mother.

Not long after we prayed we saw a van pull up from the health department. Now, usually when the health department comes to your facility it is not a good thing. I met the lady at the door and she explained that she had gotten one of our ministry brochures at a community outreach and had been trying to get by our center and finally made it that day. She said, "Do you need formula?" She had been getting formula and was not able to use it all and wanted to share with us. Her van was full of formula!

We were able to help that young mom that day and we continue to help young moms every single day. We call this "the loaves and fishes," as the formula continues to come and we continue to give it to those in need. God supplies all of our needs!

In fact, God supplies our needs so specifically that one of our volunteers shared recently that the APRC reaches even to Arizona. She told me that her grandson had a baby and the only formula the baby could drink was soy formula. The APRC had received soy formula in our shipments so we sent them on to her grandson for his baby. The amazing thing about this formula story is that once our volunteer's great-grandchild no longer needed the soy formula, it stopped coming in our shipment! God knows far better than we do how much formula we need, what kind we need, and how long we need it!

WHY ARE YOU HERE?

We had been open about six months when I had some people from the community come to visit me. I was excited that they were coming with the hopes that we could work together.

When they came, their first question was, "Why are you here?"

"Excuse me? Why am I here? There are 50,000 students just two blocks from our pregnancy resource center. That is why we are here."

"Well, there are only so many donors in Austin," I was told. Really? The concern was money? God is my supply, not man. Lives are at stake and we must answer the call and go! I shared with them that I would send donors to them. I did not believe that we had met every donor and that we should give everyone an opportunity to invest in life.

To bring unity and tear down the walls of division, I formed the Austin Area Life Affirming Coalition (AALAC). I wanted it to sound like AFLAC so people would remember, and it worked! We met once a month, and still do, at different ministries and organizations where we prayed together and served and supported one another with the goal of tearing down the walls of territory and competition. AALAC has been recognized by a resolution in the Texas House of Representatives for a network of pro-life organizations who are working together for the good of our community. We now have 50 non-profits in our coalition. I truly believe God is pleased with our unity and He is blessing beyond our greatest hopes, dreams, and imaginations (Ephesians 3:20-21).

TIME TO BUY

After four years of leasing our facility, I received a call from our building owner that the sorority next door wanted to buy our place. He said that in our lease he was to give us a 30-day notice. I shared with him that we wanted to buy the facility. He asked, "What collateral do you have?"

I thought about it a minute and said, "We have a sonogram machine." He laughed.

He asked, "What are you willing to offer for the facility?"

I had never negotiated for such a project before, but answered him, "$650,000." He laughed again.

He asked, "How about $950,000?"

I said, "$750,000."

He said, "I will sell to you for $750,000 IF you can raise $30,000 in 30 days as a down payment."

I prayed and asked the Lord for His word to move forward. He took me to Psalm 37:23, *"The steps of a man are established by the Lord, when He delights in his way; though he fall, he shall not be cast headlong, for the Lord upholds his hand. I have been young, and now am old, yet I have not seen the righteous forsaken or his children begging for bread. He is ever lending generously, and his children become a blessing."* And Psalm 37:34 *"Wait for the Lord and keep His way, and He will exalt you to inherit the land; you will look on when the wicked are cut off."*

That is all I needed! I went to work. I sent out an email to our current support base, letting them know that our facility was going to be sold to the sorority next door, but we had the option to buy if we could raise $30,000 in 30 days. I really thought I would need to make lots of calls and hold lots of meetings. Literally, immediately after the email went out, people started calling and wanting to make donations to raise the $30,000. We were able to raise $30,000 in less than two weeks' time. It was totally amazing! People were walking checks into the center to make sure we had what we needed.

I called the building owner and let him know we had raised our $30,000 and were ready to move forward to purchase the facility. He arranged an owner finance option with us and we immediately moved into building ownership. We again saw the faithfulness of God!

ENLARGING OUR TERRITORY AGAIN

After being open for a brief six months we began getting contacted by people in the community needing our services. The Austin area covers a lot of miles, and these people were not close to us. Plus, Austin is famous for traffic jams and getting to downtown Austin from the suburbs could be a challenge. As I prayed about what we should do, the Scripture that came to me was to go to the highways and byways. I had researched and knew that the best plan was to begin new pregnancy resource centers in all of these areas and develop separate 501(c)3 organizations. Others had differing opinions on the structure for these new centers, but I knew we were to form separate organizations.

I am reminded of the center in Leander, Texas. We held a community informational meeting and 21 people attended. We set an opening date for six months from that date. We found a facility that was a former pharmacy, but was totally stripped down to an open room with no offices or anything finished inside.

We contacted an architect who donated his services, and he designed the pregnancy center for us. We held another meeting to let the people know we were making progress. We shared the facility layout with them, and the architect had projected that we would need $25,000 for the build-out of the facility. We took up a collection that night of $2,500.

We went to work to contact people in the community with the various resources that we needed. Specifically, we needed 50 sheets of drywall to build the offices. I went to a drywall company and shared with them what we were planning to do and that we needed 50 sheets of drywall. Not only did they donate the 50 sheets of drywall, they delivered it and sent two men to put the walls up! It was amazing!

We were able to get the mud so we taped and floated. We painted. Then, as we were ready for the specific building materials such as lighting and carpet, I was contacted by a demolition company who said they were scheduled to demolish a $1 million house but before they did the demolition, if we could take the weekend, we could go in and get whatever we needed to build the pregnancy resource center.

With a group of volunteers, we went to the house. It was astonishing! We were blessed with very expensive crown molding, light fixtures, cabinets, shelving, carpet and more to completely finish the building of the pregnancy resource center! These were all top of the line resources, too. We actually gathered enough supplies to build three other pregnancy resource centers!

We held our grand opening on the exact day we had planned six months earlier AND we still had $2,500 in the bank! God's unmistakable hand has truly GIVEN!

EXTRAORDINARY SUPPORT OF CENTRAL TEXAS PASTORS

I have learned that as we follow the Lord and His timing that everything will fall into place. We have always been very blessed to have the support of area pastors. I am so very grateful to Dr. David Smith and the Austin Baptist Association for allowing consistent introduction of the Austin Pregnancy Resource Center at their monthly meetings.

I think of Pastor John Abraham with Rosanky Baptist Church, Dr. Ken Baldwin with Kinney Avenue Christian Fellowship, Pastor Trey Kent with Northwest Fellowship, Great Hills Baptist Church, Bannockburn Baptist Church, Terri Road Baptist Church, Oak Meadows Baptist Church, and then enlarging to St. Francis Anglican Church, and so many, many more.

One Tuesday night we were having an APRC Board meeting and a prayer team wanted to come to the center and pray. As we were meeting upstairs, I went downstairs to get something from my office and met the prayer team from Victory Christian Center. I was focused on getting back upstairs to the board meeting, but Pastor Sue Boss, the wife of Pastor Lee Boss, stopped me and laid hands on my head and prayed. I'll admit I thought that was strange, but I was appreciative.

They became a partner of the APRC, and Pastor Lee and Sue became family to me. I was blessed to be under their leadership and learn and grow through the years. Pastor Lee went on to Heaven in 2014, and I thank God for his legacy and the hope of one day seeing him again.

ST. DAVID'S PARTNERSHIP

As the Austin Pregnancy Resource Center began to grow, we began to have more and more need for doctors to send our clients to for good healthcare. I started praying, asking God to show me who we could connect with.

One Friday afternoon I received a call from the Chief Nursing Officer from St. David's Medical Center. She was asking if there was a need for good healthcare for our APRC clients. She was new to town, and really believed that God had placed her in this position to help His work.

We set up a tour of the APRC and a meeting. She brought the director of their hospital's women's services with her. We had a great meeting. From that meeting she took the information to the Chief Executive Officer for the entire hospital, along with the Chief Financial Officer. They saw what the needs were in our community and developed a specific program for clients of pregnancy resource centers to receive the health care that they need.

A 1-800 number was set up that we can give to our clients. When our clients call this number, they reach one person who knows that the call is coming from a pregnancy resource center. She then sets them up with a private doctor within two weeks of their call. They also pay an office on the hospital campus to assist clients with applying for health care coverage.

I am truly in awe at how specifically God always answers if we will simply specifically give to Him all of our heart's goals and desires. What is amazing to me is that this is truly His work, and He is waiting for us to come to Him to be obedient and available as a conduit to accomplish His work.

FEDERAL LAWSUIT

I will never forget where I was and what day it was when I received a call from an *Austin American Statesman* reporter. It was Good Friday, and the APRC was closed in remembrance of that day. I had gone to Chuy's, one of my favorite Mexican restaurants, for lunch and my phone rang.

When I answered it, the person on the other end of the call announced that she was a reporter with the *Austin American Statesman* and she would like a statement from me with regard to the new City Ordinance that the City of Austin was preparing to approve.

This was the very first time I had heard of such a thing. I knew nothing about it at all! So, as I have learned and studied how Jesus would handle such a confrontation, I asked her to read the new ordinance to me. I was praying as she read to me and asking God, "What should I do?"

When she finished reading the ordinance to me it was clear that I was to ask her some questions first. So, I said to her, "I will be happy to answer your questions if you will answer some of mine first." She agreed. "Help me understand how anyone could come against an organization serving their community with excellence, not taking any government money and not charging their clients. How could anyone come against us?"

She paused before answering and then said she did not know. I said, "Well, when you can answer this question I'll be happy to answer yours." She called me back six times that day and each time I gave her more questions. Near the end of the day she asked if I would just help her write the article as she had to get a story out. I was happy to do so. We were on the front page of the *Austin American Statesman* with a very good article on who we are and what we do.

The City of Austin unanimously passed the ordinance. The ordinance stated that we were to post a sign outside of our facility of services we do not do: *"We do not refer for abortion and we do not refer for contraception."*

We held a board meeting to discuss what we should do. I was really struggling, because I did not want to file a lawsuit against the city in which I serve; however, this was the only way to combat such an ordinance. The ordinance is a nationwide strategy of National Abortion Rights Action League, NARAL, to come against, and eventually shut down pregnancy resource centers. The year was 2010, and the nationwide strategy started in Baltimore, Maryland, and came to Austin, Texas, and was headed to San Francisco, California, and then on to New York, New York.

We held another board meeting. I was still struggling as to what to do. We were being contacted by law firms from around the country. I was also getting emails from pastors, community leaders, and national leaders from around the nation to just simply post the sign. After all, we were not referring for abortion or contraception, so what was the big deal? The big deal was that to post the sign would be to give up ground. I was not willing to do that. So, my only option was to file a lawsuit against the City of Austin, the city in which God had called me to serve.

As I was preparing to go into the third APRC board meeting I was calling out to God, "What should we do?" As He always does to give me an answer, He took me to His Word. I opened the Bible to Isaiah 10: 1-2: *"Woe to those who decree iniquitous decrees, and the writers who keep writing oppression, to turn aside the needy from justice and to rob the poor of my people of their right, that widows may be their spoil, and that they may make the fatherless their prey!"* And then He took me to the story of David and Goliath. In this story David ran quickly to the battle and was not afraid. I knew I needed to lay aside my fear and trust in the Lord to stand against this injustice!

As I went into the third board meeting, one of the lead attorneys for us with the law firm of Liberty Institute was there. I shared, again, the struggle I was having in filing a lawsuit against the city in which I serve. He then explained to me that this would not be a lawsuit in local court, but the lawsuit would be in federal court and could be used to protect pregnancy resource centers around the country. Other pregnancy center directors had been calling me to ask that I stop what was happening from NARAL in Austin so that it would not come to their city.

We voted to move forward to file the lawsuit. I had never been in a lawsuit before. I did not know what to expect. I started getting calls from attorneys, requesting interrogatories. I didn't even know what that was. However, just as David, I knew where the battle was and I chose to keep my eyes on my Lord Who fights the battles for us.

When the news hit that we were standing our ground and filing a lawsuit to counter the ordinance, attacks began. We had graffiti all over our pregnancy center, signs knocked down, dead birds placed along the front of our property, etc.

I called in prayer warriors and asked them to come anoint the property and facility with oil, and pray for this warfare to stop, and to take our God-given authority. After the prayer team came, all of the above-listed attacks stopped! We do have tools and armor that God has given us to stand in these times of warfare.

THE TRIAL

The day came for the deposition. I had never been in a deposition before. As I went into the room there was a large conference table with attorneys on either side. There was a camera focused directly on me and a court reporter sitting next to me recording everything I said.

When the attorney who was for abortion began questioning me, it was grueling. It was accusatory. It was manipulative. It was intimidating. She took three breaks so she could regroup and try her best to get me to break down. Each time my attorneys and I went into the conference room for a break, I was told what I needed to say, what I should not say, etc. I felt like I was in a scene from the movie "Rocky"! You know - the one where they take a break and Rocky is given a drink of water while his trainer tells him all the things he needs to know to fight better. I kept asking, "Is someone praying?"

I recall at one point in my deposition that one of our attorneys and the abortion attorney began arguing over an issue. As they argued I was praying. The abortion attorney stopped and looked down at the table as if she were exhausted. She then looked up and over at me and said, "I did not mean that about you." I don't even know what she said, but I did see a glimpse that she saw something different in me that she respected.

We moved into the trial. It was just like you see on television. As I went up to be sworn in, I noticed I was not sworn in on the Bible. The first attorney to question me was Erin. Erin, at the time, was a junior attorney for Liberty Institute.

I must pause and share with you the story of Erin. When we first opened the APRC in 2005, Erin was a student at the University of Texas in Austin. She was President of Pro-Life Advocates, a student organization on campus. She was dating a young man named Jordan, at the time.

I specifically remember talking with Erin when she was a student, and sharing with her to get her law degree because we might need her as an attorney one day. Erin served as a student representative on our Board of Directors, and I wanted to be an encouragement to her.

Erin and Jordan went on to graduate from the University of Texas School of Law and moved to Boston to graduate law school. They graduated and moved to Dallas, Texas, their hometown. They got married and, unbeknownst to me, Erin began working as a junior attorney at Liberty Institute.

So, in our significant federal lawsuit five years later, Erin was the junior attorney asking me the questions in our trial. God wowed me again! I rejoice at God and how He always goes ahead to prepare the way for us as we trust in Him!

We went on through the trial and when it came time for the abortion attorney to question me, the judge asked her how long her questioning of me would take. Her answer was that my questioning was the shortest.

We finished with the trial and then we waited. And waited. And waited. Finally, in 2013, we heard that Judge Lee Yaekel had made his decision and he had decided that the City Ordinance was unconstitutional. It came against our religious liberties and our free speech. He took his decision a step further in that the City of Austin was ordered to pay all attorney fees! Wow! We had seven attorneys working on our case nearly around the clock! It came to a $1 million bill! Wow again! When the mediation was all said and done, the City of Austin wrote a check to our attorneys for $480,000! It is true – God truly does fight our battles for us if we are willing to step out in faith!

THE STRATEGIC YEAR – 2013

The year 2013 was a very strategic year for the LIFE movement. I truly believe that there was a break in the spiritual stronghold in 2013! Why? Because 2013 marked the 40th year of Roe vs. Wade in our nation. I believe God still moves very methodically in

His numbers and ways of doing things. His ways are not our ways and His thoughts are not our thoughts.

In 2013, there was a major battle going on at the Texas State Capitol. A new bill was written labeled House Bill 2, or HB2, that would require abortion facilities to come up to ambulatory surgical facility standards and ban all abortions past the 20th week of gestation. This bill, that would become law, would be significant in that it would also impact other states.

I find it unthinkable that when I moved to Austin, Texas, in 1997 there had been no pro-life laws passed in the State of Texas since 1985. As I stated earlier, I believe prayer is the foundation for all of these major changes in our state and nation that we are seeing.

Prayer warriors from all over the nation came in by the busloads to pray at our State Capitol. It truly was the revelation of light and dark, right before our eyes. We were part of writing history! At one point, we who stood for LIFE, all dressed in blue, went up to the second floor of the Capitol rotunda to begin singing "Amazing Grace" and fill the atmosphere with His presence. Those who stood for abortion, dressed in orange, went up to the third floor of the Capitol rotunda and began chanting "Hail Satan, Hail Satan." We refused to be intimidated, and we began to sing "Amazing Grace" even louder. We stood our ground and they eventually went home.

We stood our ground to see HB2 voted into law. It has been challenged in every court and is currently being heard at the Supreme Court level. I truly believe, as we made our presence known and prayer warriors came from all over the country, that something in the spirit realm broke. We literally saw a paradigm shift toward LIFE and entered into a new day! We look to God, not to people, to fight and win our battles!

I believe in this new day we will see men and women who have experienced abortion find their healing and their places in standing for LIFE! I believe in this new day we will see youth and young adults rise up and take their rightful positions to lead our nation back to Godly principles and value of LIFE.

MEETING JULIE ZIGLAR NORMAN

In 2012 our board began looking at our strengths and areas where we could use improvement. We continue to find great favor with area churches and with non-profits as we have developed our Austin Area Life Affirming Coalition (AALAC). We have grown AALAC to 50 non-profits that meet regularly and pray together and support one another.

The area we needed improvement in was connection with the business world. I had not attended a national conference for several years after starting the APRC because I simply did not have the time, so I decided to attend the Heartbeat International Conference being held in Dallas, Texas. In 2013, Karen, our office manager, had just started working full-time with us and I wanted her to see the work of pregnancy centers on a national basis. I had also been invited to lead a workshop at the conference.

So, we went. You know how it is when you have so many things to do that you just do what you need to do and leave. That was my frame of mind at that conference. I had fulfilled all of my commitments, such as leading the workshop, meeting and greeting directors at the Ambassador Speaker's Bureau booth, and being interviewed for a video for Heartbeat. We were packing up and literally walking out, and in walks a new speaker I had not met.

What is interesting, is that I had asked Gloria with Ambassador Speaker's Bureau the night before who might be a good fit for our speaker for our banquet in the fall. We had discussed some potential people I could contact.

So, when this new speaker walked in, I turned around to see who she was. I asked Gloria. Gloria quickly took me over and introduced me to Julie. I began sharing with Julie that our board was interested in reaching more of the business world. She said she could assist us with that, since her father, motivational icon Zig Ziglar, had a great reputation in the business community across America.

Wonderful! I could see an answer to prayer for reaching the business world, but I was also delighted to ultimately find a true friend who God could use to help me grow in Him. I am honored and privileged to walk through life with Julie and watch God do amazing things, and I am forever grateful for her friendship!

ZIGLAR LEGACY CERTIFICATION TRAINING

Julie and her family wanted, very much, to keep their father's legacy alive, so they developed certification trainings, the first of which I was honored to go through to become a Ziglar Legacy Certified Trainer. I remember being on a webinar and listening to the explanation of the Certified training and knowing that 2,500 people were on the webinar from all over the world. I didn't think I would have a chance to participate in something that awesome!

After the webinar I received a call from the Ziglar headquarters asking me if I would be interested in submitting my application. I was interested, but had no idea how I would be selected. They were planning to select 25 people. I submitted my application and was accepted!

Because I took the week-long training class, I have the opportunity to deliver Zig Ziglar's training on: *Goal Setting and Achievement, Personal Development and Winning Relationships*.

Tom Ziglar has become my business coach, Cindy Ziglar has become my friend, as has their mother, Jean Ziglar, the "Redhead"! I never had the opportunity to meet Zig Ziglar on this earth, but I look forward to meeting him one day in Heaven. I have become part of the Ziglar family, and could not be more honored, privileged, and blessed! My heart is forever grateful!

Ariel "Ari" Love DeVillez

Have you ever seen the love of God poured out to you through a dog? After meeting Julie, I quickly learned of her love for animals. I thought that was really cool, as I love animals, too. I had not had a pet since moving to Texas, simply because of the demands of my schedule and travel. It was fun to be surrounded by Julie's four happy dogs.

One day a skinny, timid, little black dog showed up at Julie's daughter's house. Julie's daughter, Amey, gave the dog food and wanted to help her, but she couldn't keep her. Julie asked a friend of hers to take care of the dog while she looked for a permanent home.

I well remember Julie calling me one day and I asked her what she was doing. She said, "I'm driving down the road with your dog." Really? Immediately, I knew she was right! I got very excited and could hardly wait to see the dog!

This was in November of 2013, just before I was to attend the first class for Ziglar Legacy Certified Training. Julie was one of the trainers that week, so I asked her husband, Jim, if he would mind taking care of the dog until the certification class was over.

I was excited to meet the dog, and even though I thought I would probably just find her a good home, I immediately fell in love with her and I prayed over a name for her. The name "Ariel" came to mind. I looked it up and Ariel means "healing;" "new beginning;" and "lion of God." Powerful!

I went with Julie to the veterinarian to have Ari checked out. The vet found an identity chip in her that traced her back to the Humane Society in Tyler, Texas, near where Amey lived. My heart sank as I thought I might not be able to keep her. However, when I called the Humane Society they said that no one had registered her and I could keep her. They had no interest in taking her back.

I was especially excited as I drove home to Evansville, Indiana, for Christmas that year. I wanted my parents to meet Ari and love her as much as I did. When we arrived, there were Christmas presents under the tree for Ari and she accepted my parents as quickly as they accepted her. She fit in immediately.

Ari has completely settled in and become such a special, confident dog. I thank God that He has taught me so many things through Ari.

I know God has taught me many things through Ari. He has taught me to always be as loving to everyone as she is to me. He has shown me how loyal she is to me, and that I should be as loyal to Him. He has taught me that as I show love to her, she has responded by becoming confident and ready to give love to others. He has taught me to slow down, as Ari likes to take many walks and play. Best of all, He has taught me to enjoy life more through her.

I took her to obedience school and she already knew all of her commands. She is a very smart dog! I know she is my dog so, naturally, I'm going to think she is the smartest dog there is, but she really is smart! She loves to go to the pregnancy center and love on everyone. We have taught her to give hugs. She goes to lots of meetings with me and greets everyone and then lies down. She brings life in a whole new way everywhere she goes!

I was preparing to teach a class at church, so I was up early. I was rubbing Ari's belly and praying when I suddenly had an "ah ha!" moment. You may know how it is when it is clear God is speaking to you. Well, He was speaking. He said, "I want you to be like Ari." I exclaimed, "What?" He said, "Ari is totally dependent on you. She would not have water or food without your provision. Ari is totally relaxed and does not worry about anything. Air loves to be with you. She follows you around the house to be in your presence. She is excited to see you. I want you to be that way with me. I want you to be totally dependent upon me. I want you to totally relax and be free of worry. I want you to love me and long to be in my presence. I want you to be with me like Ari is with you." Seeing my relationship with God this way has totally transformed how I look at everything in my life!

I thank God every day for Ari, and for allowing me to have her to hug and to pet and to spoil. I pray to give her a great home of love and joy and that we will share many adventures together in life.

GOING MOBILE

In April of 2013, I told our volunteers it was time for us to begin our Mobile Pregnancy Resource Center. I didn't fully understand what that meant at the time, but I had seen that other pregnancy centers around the country had begun mobile units, and I like to stay on the forefront when it comes to saving lives, both literally and eternally.

Our board discussed it at length and had the idea to purchase an ambulance and transform it into a mobile sonogram unit. Other groups had RVs that they were using, and/or big buses. I mentioned the idea at a community meeting and that we were praying about it.

Two months later, in June of 2013, I received a call from a fellow community leader. He told me he was at an auction and they had good deals on ambulances. He asked how much I would be willing to pay for one. I shared with him that the money was not in the account but that $12,000-$15,000 was what I was thinking. He called me back within 30 minutes and said that he had purchased an ambulance for us. I reminded him that we did not have the money in the account. He said, "That's ok, I'll give you 30 days and I'll have no problem selling this vehicle." Man! I didn't know what to do. So, I took Karen, our office manager, with me and we went and laid hands on it and prayed.

I left for a week of vacation with my niece. While I was on vacation I ended up getting a serious sunburn. At the end of that week, I was in bed with fever and a great deal of pain when the phone rang. It was Karen. She said, "Lori, we received a large check in the mail today. It is $26,492!" I asked, "Are you sure it is made out to us?" Amazing how we question God, even after we pray and ask and say we believe!

When I called to find out where the check had come from, I saw that it was from a foundation in Missouri from an anonymous donor! Isn't that just like God?! He knew we would need $12,500 to pay for the vehicle, $4800 to pay for the vehicle wrap, $10,000 to pay for the mobile sonogram machine, which comes to $27,300! Only God could have planned this one out the way He did.

We transformed the ambulance so that it no longer looks medical. We added carpet in the back, curtains, and a mobile bathroom. We have all of our material support, such as formula, diapers and clothing, in the compartments where they used to have the medical supplies. Inside we have our brochures and the Bibles that we give away. It is perfect!

We named the mobile unit Marvie D, because he came to us in a marvelous way and he delivers! Marvie D gets invited to Central Texas community events all the time.

We have shared what and how we do our mobile services with other pregnancy resource centers around the country, and now God has duplicated Marvie D several times over as other centers have gone to their communities and shared the vision. I love how God uses His people and His plan to accomplish His work!

BUILDING REFINANCE

Have you ever had fear hit you so hard that you couldn't breathe? That is what happened to me in July of 2014. I was driving to Dallas and received a call from Karen, saying that we had received a certified letter from an attorney on behalf of our current APRC facility owner that he was demanding $780,000 in 10 days or we were to move out! Seriously! I was shocked! What were we going to do?

I knew we would need an attorney. I called a friend of mine who is an attorney and had served on our board. She let me know that she was no longer practicing law but could give me a referral.

Once again, I was reminded of how God goes ahead of us. I had gotten an email a few months prior, asking me if I would assist a college student in writing a paper. I get requests for this all the time. We were able to get the information the student needed and, at the end of the project, his dad said if I ever needed anything to let him know. I was appreciative and grateful and didn't think any more about it.

When Mary sent the referral, the name sounded familiar. So, I research my emails for the name and it was the name of the dad of the student that I had helped a few months prior. When I looked up who he was, not only is he an attorney, but he is a real estate attorney! God goes ahead of us and knows the details we need!

Immediately I began praying and the song that came to my mind was, *"Jesus is the Answer for the world today. Above Him there is no other; Jesus is the way."* One of the choruses to that song is: *"I know you have questions in the corners of your mind. Traces of discouragement and peace you cannot find. Just in case you don't know the Word of God is true and everything He's promised, He will do it for you."* Perfect! I began to build confidence.

Within that same week I was recording for a radio show and received a text to call one of our pastors' wives, Nancy Giacolone. When I called her she shared that she and Father Len had been watching the 700 Club and that at the end of the program Pat Robertson had been praying and he stopped and said, "There is a financial need. It is $700,000, it is a house. I'm to tell you God is meeting the need!" Amazing! How totally incredible is that?!

As I prayed, what I heard is that "it just takes one." One what? One person? One check? One organization? What?

We disputed the letter from the owner which gave us more time. We were able to delay until October 1, 2014. So, we had August and September to come up with $780,000! I sent out an email to our supporters, letting them know what was going on, and asked them to spread the word. At the same time, we applied with Frost Bank and were approved for $500,000.

Then one day I received a call that one person wanted to meet the need. He wanted to wire the money and only required a 2% interest rate. Astounding! We began the paperwork. At the same time, Pastor Lee was very ill and on September 25, 2014, he passed on to Heaven. On the day of Pastor Lee's memorial services, we were signing paperwork and contacting the bank to have the funds wired. It was 4:45 p.m. when I received word that $775,000 had been wired to relieve the note and save our facility. Incredible! Only God BUT God did it all! God touched someone I have never met, and who has never seen our facility, to help us. I am bowled over once again!

MEETING PASTOR ED

I had been meeting with the Austin Ambassadors for World Vision, Sherry and David Thompson. I thought I could help them with raising some funds if I could contact Stephanie Fast, who had been a world spokesperson for World Vision for ten years.

When I contacted Stephanie, she said that she was no longer speaking for World Vision, but had begun speaking for an organization called Loving Shepherd Ministries. I shared with her that I understood, but really would like for her to come and speak for Sherry and David Thompson to raise money for the orphans. After all, aren't we all here for the children?

Stephanie agreed to come and speak for our APRC Fall Extravaganza and then she could meet David and Sherry. That was the year I actually had two keynote speakers for our Extravaganza, Shawn Carney with Coalition for Life, and Stephanie Fast.

While Stephanie was in Austin, I learned more about what she was doing with Loving Shepherd Ministries, and she invited me to go on a vision trip to Haiti to meet Pastor Ed Schwartz, Founder of Loving Shepherd Ministries, and see the children and the work they are doing in Haiti. I agreed to go.

That first trip to Haiti was inspiring. It was so very eye-opening for me to see the children and the poor through the eyes of Jesus. I wept most of the trip.

When I returned I was sharing with many people what I had seen while in Haiti. I was surprised at the responses from some of the people I spoke with. They shared with me that we have poor children in the United States. Yes, we do; however, nothing like what is in Haiti. I know there are needs everywhere, and I know that God is pleased when we bless those in need.

The Scripture is so powerful in addressing the orphans: James 1:27 *"Religion that God our Father accepts as pure and faultless is this: to look after orphans and widows in their distress and to keep oneself from being polluted by the world."*

We at the Austin Pregnancy Resource Center are continuing to partner with Loving Shepherd Ministries and Pastor Ed, and seeing great results in Haiti. We will see what was once, one of the poorest nations in the Western Hemisphere, one day turned around because of the work of Loving Shepherd Ministries.

AMPLIFY AUSTIN – *TAKE BACK AUSTIN*

In 2015 we had an interesting opportunity to make a stand for the Gospel. For the prior three years, the Austin non-profit organizations had come together to raise funds through a 24-hour online giving campaign. However, that most recent year there was an added limitation: You could not share the Gospel with the funds raised; you could not use it for a facility; you could not use it for administrative costs, only for social services; and again, you could not share the Gospel in those services. It was very specific and very targeted.

I made some calls to other non-profit leaders in the community to see if they planned to participate. They said they did not like the new policies, but were trying to find a way to make it work.

It simply was not right. So, I called a board meeting for us to discuss what we should do. We decided we would not participate. I prayed and asked the Lord for His Word on what to do. He took me to Psalm 55:9 *"Destroy, O Lord, divide their tongues; for I see violence and strife in the city."* And verse 21, *"His speech was smooth as butter, yet war was in his heart; his words were softer than oil, yet there were drawn swords. Cast your burden on the Lord, and He will sustain you; He will never permit the righteous to be moved."* I wrote an email to our supporters to let them know that we would not be participating in Amplify Austin, but instead would be running our own 24-hour online giving campaign and calling it *Take Back Austin*.

My email was forwarded to the CEO of Amplify Austin who, in turn, called me. He was very upset and asked me several times to rescind my words. I told him I would rescind my words only if he changed the policy. We will not compromise sharing the Gospel in anything we do. He said he could not do that and would not be able to make any changes until after the campaign.

The next day I was driving to the pregnancy center and thought it was important that the community know what was going on. I called one of our attorneys to see if they could inform the media. He said if it was a government situation they could, but this was a private foundation.

But God wanted the community to know, and when I arrived at the pregnancy center that day, a reporter from the *Austin American Statesman* was on the line waiting for me. I spoke with him and shared with him our viewpoint on the situation.

We received a front page article the next morning in the *Austin American Statesman.* I then received calls from corporate sponsors and other non-profits. They were all going to pull out.

On the following Monday, Amplify Austin announced they were changing their policies and the CEO was rescinding his words.

I have learned if I am willing, available, and obedient to whatever God calls me to, and I'm willing to step out of my comfort zone, that God is always faithful to meet me there on the water and accomplish His will in every situation. We can impact our culture. We do not have to allow our culture to control us. My heart is forever grateful!

ISRAEL AND THE UKRAINE

Have you ever had a desire to go to Israel? I have, for many years! It is one of those dreams that you keep before you and pray that one day it will become reality. I'd like to share with you how that dream became a reality in 2015, and about the added trip to the Ukraine.

When I was invited to go on the trip, the first question was, "How much will it cost?" The amount was $5,000 to go on both trips. It is amazing how the first money came. I had done some work a while back and had not been paid. Then the group I had worked with contacted me to apologize that they had missed paying me and the amount was $4,300! I only needed $700 more! Sweet! I was praying about the remaining $700 and left the care with the Lord and went on about my day.

Then, I had the thought that I needed to go see my friend and insurance agent, Bill Muench. I was so surprised. Really? I usually just email or call him. This morning I was to go see him. I decided to go over to his office, which I had never done before. His wife was also there that day. We began visiting about all the amazing things going on at the APRC. I shared with them that I was planning to go to Israel and the Ukraine, and that I was praying for the remaining $700. Then, as I was getting ready to leave, they said, "Let's pray." After we prayed, his wife, Brenda, said, "You need to write Lori a check."

Her husband asked, "Ok, for how much?" And she said, "Seven hundred dollars for her Israel/Ukraine trip!" What a blessing! God had answered specifically and His people had been obedient to hear His leading! As usual, how can I not be moved to the point of tears!

It was the trip of a lifetime! I did everything from being baptized in the Jordan River to riding a camel, to floating on the Dead Sea. One question I had before I went to Israel was: "What is the connection in the heart of God between Israel and LIFE?" We were on the Mount of Beatitudes and I asked the question again. God clearly answered, "It is my covenant." We serve a covenant-keeping God! Covenant – a word that has become foreign in our society today, but a word that is very serious to our Lord.

The trip to the Ukraine was even more special than I had imagined it would be. I was able to spend time with the older girls at an orphanage there and talk with them about life and their plans, hopes, and dreams. We stood in a circle at the end of the visit and made a purity pact. God is God anywhere we go, and people are people who need the same thing: love, acceptance, and hope. I praise God that we carry the answer everywhere we go and can influence and change our atmosphere just by speaking the Name of Jesus!

APRC NEW CARPET

God cares about the little things and He is the best decorator I know! We began speaking about needing new carpet for the APRC as we were going into our 11th year of ministry. With nearly 2,000 clients a year, and all the people who came in with them, there had been a lot of traffic on our carpet and it was beginning to look threadbare.

I believe it is important, as you may have figured out by now, that when we represent our Lord we should represent Him in excellence. Just like in the early days at the unwed mother's home, I knew we weren't doing that.

One of our volunteers asked her church leaders if they would consider serving the APRC when they went out, as they traditionally did, on the fifth Sunday to serve the community.

The fifth Sunday was going to be the end of January. It wasn't until mid-January when they came to look at the facility to see if they could help. I know it usually takes a good bit of time to order carpet and installations, especially for the size job that we had for two floors.

They asked me what color and kind of carpet I wanted. I told them I would trust God on that, as I know He is the best decorator. Not only were they able to get a very nice grade carpet, and the right color, but all of the materials were donated, as well as the labor, to install it, and everything came in right on time! The church had allocated $3,000 for the carpet, but since everything was donated we were also able to get other items and repairs done. I love His precise and perfect provision! I'm forever grateful!

MY MOVE

God orders our steps. He truly does give us everything we need if we will just follow Him.

All through the year I was praying and thinking that I should move from my home. God blessed me with a brand new home and I had been the only one who lived in it for 12 years - well, with the exception of Ari, who came into my life in 2013.

I had done many Internet searches and one day I received a call from a realtor, Wendy, asking if she could help me find the home I was looking for. Surprised me! How does that happen? I don't fully understand technology and how it all works.

I shared with her the items on my list that God had asked me to make. She put some information together and sent me some possible properties. Right away I found a place I thought I would like. We met over at the house to walk through it. I thought it was great. She then put me in touch with a mortgage lender and with another member of her team who could help sell my current home. I was amazed that everything I needed was right there, waiting for me.

I made an offer on the home and they countered with an amount that was within my predetermined price range. So we began moving forward with the loan application. In the midst of our planning and staging and showings, someone else offered a lot more money and had cash, so I did not get the house. I was ok with that because I fully trusted the Lord, that He had the best for me. The Scripture that He keeps reminding me of is that He perfects those things that concern me.

At the same time, I received a cash offer on my current home. I was excited! But that offer quickly fell through, so we were back to more showings. One thing I have learned in the selling of a home process is that the showing times are the most challenging. Ari and I felt like we lived out of our car for three weeks!

We received more offers and then the perfect offer came through. So, Wendy and I began searching for a home for me to move to. Wendy was funny when she said she did not want me to be without a home.

We walked through many homes, but the last home we walked through was THE ONE. A brand new home with a huge back yard on a greenbelt. I would be getting away from traffic, people, noise, and have a quiet, private place to call home.

In the process, I was going to go to the pregnancy center and called to talk with Karen before going in. I shared with her I was going to pick up some moving boxes on my way. She said, "Wait, we have moving boxes!" One of our volunteers brought them in. She said she didn't know why, but felt she should leave them at the pregnancy center. She had no idea I was planning to move! I love how God provides down to the details of moving boxes!

What is so cool about this whole process is that I ended up with amazing new friends. Casey, who walked me through selling my old home; Wendy, who saw to it that I did, in fact, have a new home to move to; and Chris, who expertly took care of securing my new home loan. I'm forever grateful to each one of them!

WHY LIFE ITSELF IS A MISSION FIELD IN THE USA

The miracles I have seen since becoming involved with Pregnancy Resource Centers happen with stunning regularity. I wish I had kept notes on all of them as they came to pass. I want you to know why I became so passionate about helping men and women choose life for their babies, and why I love helping those who chose abortion discover that God loves them still. As you read the following, I believe the importance of this mission field in America will become unmistakably clear, as will the reason I was so excited to discover that God was sending me to my own country.

In John 10:10 we read, *"The thief comes to steal, kill and destroy, but I have come that they may have LIFE and have it abundantly."* On January 22, 1973, the US Supreme Court declared abortion upon demand legal in this nation with the Roe vs. Wade case. The Doe vs. Bolton case, the case heard the same day as Roe vs. Wade, not only made abortion upon demand legal, but made it legal through all nine months of pregnancy.

What do pregnancy resource centers do? I'm so very glad you asked. I say we mainly do these things:

We live out Matthew 25:37 *"Then the righteous will answer him, 'Lord, when did we see you hungry and feed you, or thirsty and give you something to drink? ^{38} When did we see you a stranger and invite you in, or needing clothes and clothe you? ^{39} When did we see you sick or in prison and go to visit you?' ^{40} "The King will reply, 'Truly I tell you, whatever you did for one of the least of these brothers and sisters of mine, you did for me.' ^{41} "Then he will say to those on his left, 'Depart from me, you who are cursed, into the eternal fire prepared for the devil and his angels. ^{42} For I was hungry and you gave me nothing to eat, I was thirsty and you gave me nothing to drink, ^{43} I was a stranger and you did not invite me in, I needed clothes and you did not clothe me, I was sick and in prison and you did not look after me.' ^{44} "They also will answer, 'Lord, when did we see you hungry or thirsty or a stranger or needing clothes or sick or in prison, and did not help you?' ^{45} "He will reply, 'Truly I tell you, whatever you did not do for one of the least of these, you did not do for me.'"*

We meet the physical needs through our clothing boutique.

We live out Psalm 139 by the powerful tool of sonography. We get to show them the amazing life being formed within them.

"For you created my inmost being; you knit me together in my mother's womb. [14] *I praise you because I am fearfully and wonderfully made; your works are wonderful, I know that full well.* [15] *My frame was not hidden from you when I was made in the secret place, when I was woven together in the depths of the earth.* [16] *Your eyes saw my unformed body; all the days ordained for me were written in your book before one of them came to be.* [17] *How precious to me are your thoughts,* [a] *God! How vast is the sum of them!* [18] *Were I to count them, they would outnumber the grains of sand - when I awake, I am still with you."*

After we show them the baby on the sonogram screen we talk with them about their life. Did you know your life also has purpose? Some have never been told that their life has purpose. They frequently weep right there in the sonogram room.

Then we share John 3:16, *"For God so loved the world that he gave his one and only Son, that whoever believes in him shall not perish but have eternal life."*

We offer them hope in Jesus. That is what makes us different from a social service agency - we offer them Jesus.

CHANGING AND SAVING LIVES

When I think of building a culture of life, I think it goes beyond the babies. It also goes to the moms and the dads. It goes to the grandmas and grandpas. It even goes to friends on the streets.

Let me tell you about a woman I will call "Rhonda." We help with a homeless outreach one Sunday a month. One Sunday when I went to serve, I met "Rhonda." She yelled at me when I asked if I could pray with her. She said, "I'm mad at God!" I said, "Tell Him. He can handle it!" She said in an even louder voice, "You didn't hear me, I said I'm mad at God!" I said, "Yes, I heard you and it is important that you tell Him because He can handle it." She stomped off, but I did give her my APRC business card and told her if she ever wanted someone to talk with, to please call.

"Rhonda" showed up at the APRC. She came into my office and said, "I'm not really mad at God. I'm hurt. I lost my two grandbabies in a car accident. Why did God take them?" We prayed and I held her while she cried.

It has been a long journey with "Rhonda," but she is now in her own apartment and off the streets. She has her own cleaning business for which we were able to provide the first cleaning supplies. It is exciting to see the love of Jesus, and how the power of His love transforms lives.

Allie also comes to mind. Allie was a senior at the University of Texas and found herself 19 weeks pregnant. She and her boyfriend went to an abortion facility to have an abortion. While she was having her sonogram, she was watching her boyfriend's face, and when she asked to see the sonogram screen to see what her boyfriend was seeing, they turned the monitor off.

She decided not to have the abortion that day because she wanted to see the sonogram. She looked online and found the APRC and came in for a sonogram. She chose life for her baby that day.

It was quite a battle even after that, however, as her boyfriend wanted nothing to do with this baby. He offered to drive her to Houston for an abortion. She finally said she was going to have the baby and the boyfriend left.

Allie graduated from the University of Texas with her baby girl by her side!

Tabitha also comes to mind. She was pregnant and scared. She had three other children and one of them was physically challenged. She went to an abortion facility to have her abortion. There were sidewalk counselors asking her to "Please have mercy!" She ignored them and went on in to have her abortion.

Inside the abortion facility they told her how much it would cost, but she didn't have the money. They gave her a number to call for financing, but the line was busy.

She finally said she needed to leave. The sidewalk counselors were still outside, and asked her if they could help. They gave her an Austin Pregnancy Resource Center (APRC) brochure and she went in for a visit that day. She said she just needed encouragement, she would need to be off work to have the baby and she needed to care for her other children.

We went to work to help her. The University Life Advocates committed to get gifts for Tabitha's other children for Christmas, and our pregnancy center covered two months of rent for her. She named the baby Emani, which is Swahili for peace, and Nevaeh, which is Heaven spelled backwards.

When Emani was little she ran happily around the APRC offices like a typical toddler. Her mom told us that only at the APRC would she do that. Any other place she clung to her momma. Emani instinctively knew she was safe at the APRC; a place that felt like home.

I especially love the story of fifteen-year-old Sarah. When she told her dad she was pregnant, he took her to an abortion facility. While she was waiting for her abortion she got scared and called her mom.

Her mom picked her up that day but didn't know what to do. They were driving around the streets of Austin and saw a billboard that said, "Pregnant? Need Help? Call 1-800-395-HELP." They called the number and went to the APRC. While there they talked through many things, and they both ended up rededicating their lives to Christ.

Sarah's baby, David, was born and on Father's Day Sunday he was dedicated to the Lord. Today David is living out His God-ordained destiny.

WHAT ELSE DO WE DO?

We also refer for adoption. The APRC had been open for six months when a client came in who was already in her sixth month of pregnancy. She had had an abortion earlier in life, and had also parented her son, but was now pregnant for a third time and wanted to place for adoption.

We had not done any adoptions at the APRC yet. I called my friend, Bev Kline at Loving Alternatives, and asked if she could help. She said she could equip me to handle the process if I would come to Loving Alternatives for training and fulfill all of the state requirements for placement.

We worked closely with Bev and her staff to help this client place her baby for adoption. Before she placed for adoption she made a video for him to see so he could one day understand why she chose adoption. It was so precious. She held his little hand and said, "I want you to hear from me why I came to this decision to place you with this amazing family. It is because I love you so much. I want you to have a mommy and a daddy. I want you to have all of the opportunities in life. It is because of my love for you that I chose to place you in this family." I am excited to tell you that this little boy spoke about his adoption before a crowd of over 600 people at our 2015 APRC Fall Extravaganza.

THERE IS EVEN MORE TO THE APRC

We offer abortion recovery Bible studies for men and women who need emotional and spiritual healing from the devastation that choosing abortion brought into their lives. Men and women who are fully restored are powerful witnesses against abortion and for life.

We work equally hard to help young people develop healthy, moral lifestyles, equipping them for the New Day!

All of the above are the reasons I know I am called to ministry in America, and, more specifically, in the Pregnancy Resource Center arena.

AS THE JOURNEY CONTINUES

I think of the song, *"Every day with Jesus, is sweeter than the day before. Every day with Jesus, I love Him more and more. Jesus saves and keeps me, and He's the one I'm living for. Every day with Jesus, is sweeter than the day before."* Oh, how true it is!

It is my prayer that, as we have spent time together through the pages of this book, you have been encouraged, inspired, and motivated to see more and more of what He will do as we draw closer and closer to Him.

There really is nothing impossible with Him. Matthew 17:20, *He replied, "Because you have so little faith. Truly I tell you, if you have faith as small as a mustard seed, you can say to this mountain, 'Move from here to there,' and it will move. Nothing will be impossible for you."*

He really does move mountains on our behalf. He is our Defender. He is our Provider. He is Love. He is Joy. He is peace that passes all understanding.

We live in a time when we must dig deep to walk by faith. Our faith is being challenged more and more. I ask the students, "Can you defend your faith when needed?" Many are not sure what that means. How do you defend your faith? How do you build a culture of life? How do you lift the Name of Jesus high? These are all questions we need to know how to clearly answer. I believe we must live out our faith through every action we take. Every action must be purposeful. We must pray and live as to see what Jesus sees. I'm asking Him to show me my judgmental thoughts and attitudes. It is amazing how He is showing me so many things. I don't want to be the same tomorrow as I am today. The only way to change is to recognize who we are and what we do, and purposely make changes in our thoughts and our actions.

I want to be so in line with Him that I see things as David did. He didn't see how big Goliath was; he saw how big his God is. He knew what His God could do because he had lived out many situations before and seen how God came through. Through the stories in this book, you can see that God has come through time and again on behalf of LIFE and the lives that depend on us. I do not take that lightly. *"Lord, I pray that everyone reading this book will come to you and ask you key questions so that your answers will draw them all closer to you. Lord, may we believe you for great and mighty things. May we believe you for the small things. May we simply believe."*

As I asked earlier in this book, do you have a dream? Has God put something deep inside of you that you know needs to happen? If so, pursue it with all you have. Don't give up on your dream. We all have purpose, an assignment, a drive for why we were created, and specific assignments to accomplish.

To God be the Glory!

With a grateful heart,

Lori DeVillez

The Assignment – Living Life Strategically

A Tribute to Pat and Gary Wayne DeVillez, Sr.

Psalm 127:4 (NIV) – "Like arrows in the hands of a warrior are children born in one's youth."

As I sit here preparing this very special tribute to my parents, Pat and Wayne DeVillez, I am overwhelmed with gratitude for the wonderful blessing they have been in my life. It is from them I learned the lesson which has proven most valuable – how to give myself away for a greater cause.

When I think of growing up, fond memories of time spent with my dad quickly flood my mind. I recall going fishing with him on my aunt and uncle's property (where my brother lives today) and catching my very first fish. I was so excited that I didn't know what to do! I wanted to run and tell someone, yet at the same time, I wanted to stay and take the fish off the hook.

A couple of my all-time favorite adventures were when we went horseback riding and when we went goose hunting. How many goose hunting chicks do you know? I remember one particular time when we were hunting, it was so cold that my dad told me to run up and down the corn fields to keep myself warm. I smile each time I think about that day! My childhood was filled with fun, and I have safely tucked those cherished memories away in the depths of my heart and my mind to hold onto forever.

I want to thank my parents for my brother, Gary Wayne DeVillez, Jr. Gary was born September 2, 1970. I will always remember that morning! My mom was screaming in pain and my dad was driving 70 miles an hour in a 35 mile-an-hour zone over the top of Mill Road Hill. I remember the first time I saw Gary. His hair was white and he was so tiny! When a friend of mine asked to hold him, I told her she couldn't. I wanted to protect my new little brother.

As the years have gone by, I have grown even fonder of my brother. I have seen how hard he works and how he uses his work as his mission field. He loves to help others and has such a giving heart.

I am forever grateful that God chose to give me an amazing brother in Gary.

Nothing could surpass dinnertime at the DeVillez's, when we all gathered around the table to enjoy a wonderful meal prepared by my mom and share the events of the day. As soon as we were done eating, my dad always finished the evening by reading the Bible to us. Family unity was built during those times, and the Biblical principles we were taught gave us a stable foundation, allowing us to deepen our relationship with God.

Christmas was always a special family event! My mom made sure everything was festive and perfect. Plus, it was a great treat to spend time in the kitchen with her, baking cookies for our family as well as many other friends and family. My dad provided us with entertainment as he opened his gifts. He would unwrap one end of the gift and try to guess what the present was and try to convince us that he knew exactly what it was without looking . . . but we knew better!

Oh, how I thank God for my mom and the example she was to me as a young girl, and for the role model she continues to be. She was always giving and giving and then giving again to help others. I have watched her countless times look for ways to bless people. She has a determination and drive in finding a solution to any problem. What a true inspiration she has been in showing me how to persevere and to help others in their time of need. There was never a task too great for her to take on. I am forever grateful for the consistency and warmth with which she filled our home and hearts.

The majority of my childhood my dad was employed at Whirlpool Corporation in Evansville, Indiana. During his employment, Whirlpool was striving to become a well-known corporation and household name. However, there were periods of times they struggled in providing a stable work environment for their employees, due to economic challenges. On several occasions, I recall my dad being on strike, and he would allow me to tag along with him to the picket line. He always worked hard, and at times picked up extra side jobs to provide for our family. Not only was he a loving father and devoted husband, but he truly modeled the example of genuinely caring for people. At work, he always offered a helping hand to his fellow co-workers. He didn't hesitate to stand up for those who felt they didn't have a voice.

All of my life I have seen my father go the extra mile. When his brother was sick, he made time to be there for him, no matter how great the challenge. My dad drove his brother to the hospital and home again, and made sure his needs were taken care of. It was very difficult as a child to watch the grief and heartache my dad experienced when his father and brother relocated to Heaven.

After the passing of Dad's father, I watched as his stepmother made poor decisions and hurtful choices, but my dad remained steadfast in his character and chose to love and serve her, honoring her position in his life as God would have him do. Though his heart had been hurt by her actions, he modeled love in its purest form by being there for her until she breathed her last breath here on earth. On one occasion, he took her dog to the groomer before taking the dog to visit her at the hospital. Now, that's going the extra mile! Dad's constant acts of kindness cultivated a heart of giving within me.

When Dad's mother became very ill and the doctors said she had only a short time to live, my dad could have chosen to leave her in a nursing home, but he didn't. He brought her home and rallied family and friends together to help care for her around the clock. Even though there were times when it became very difficult to maintain all the responsibilities, he would not abandon his post and allow his mother to be alone during her illness.

I'll never forget the day I received a call and was told that my grandma had been non-responsive for three days. I had accepted an opportunity to be a keynote speaker at a national conference in Louisville, Kentucky, and decided to fulfill my obligation before heading home. I left promptly after speaking and drove straight to Evansville, Indiana, to see her.

As I entered her room, I went over to my grandmother's bedside and gently touched her arm. I noticed that her fingers moved and as I spoke these words, "I love you," her lips began to move. It was a miracle - she was trying to respond to me. For three days she was completely non-responsive, yet at that moment something special happened. It was as though she had been waiting for me, to say goodbye. Thirty minutes quickly went by - then a gentle peace filled the room as she was ushered into the arms of Jesus.

Through life's journey there has been much love, laughter, sadness and tears. I wouldn't trade any of it! My parents have always been solid. They have taught us not to lean on our own understanding, but to trust in God. I am forever grateful to have parents who made our home a house of prayer and a place where Jesus was head of the household. I've seen them lead with integrity and love, and I have watched as they served their family, friends, church, co-workers, enemies, and the community throughout my childhood and adult life. What a great and mighty legacy they continue to prepare for their children and grandchildren.

Dad and Mom, thank you for who you are and who you've taught me to be, not with mere words, but by your actions. You have displayed to me how to love others unconditionally.

I appreciate all the times you disciplined me and how you directed me with your wisdom and advice. You've reminded me, *"We have not, because we ask not."* What a core value that has been to me as I lead a ministry today. But most of all, thank you for allowing me to dream big and for supporting my vision. I value and cherish every single memory and every ounce of love you have given me.

I love you, Mom and Dad!

Forever in my heart,

Your daughter, Lori

Biography

Lori DeVillez

Equipped with a Bachelor of Arts degree in psychology/social work from the University of Southern Indiana, and a background in social work, public administration, and missions, Lori DeVillez began her career path of serving pregnancy centers in 1992. From her first position, which provided on-the-job medical training, to leadership of both a pregnancy center and a maternity home, Lori advanced to becoming President of The Heidi Group, an Austin, Texas-based organization that assists women's pregnancy resource centers.

From 1997-2005 Lori traveled the nation on behalf of The Heidi Group, helping centers develop strategic ministry and providing training in all aspects of pregnancy resource center management. Lori's teachings included superior management and administrative practices, strategic planning for boards of directors, personnel training and certification, fund-raising, development of new centers, how to have great conferences and offer continuing education, as well as developing successful media campaigns to reach women in crisis and more.

Lori discovered she had a heart for the 100,000-plus students of the University-dense city of Austin, Texas, shortly after she moved there in 1997. Her vision for a pregnancy center adjacent to the UT campus was realized in January of 2005 when the Austin Pregnancy Resource Center became a reality. In March of that year, Lori DeVillez became the executive director of that facility and has planted 12 more pregnancy resource centers in the Austin area to date.

Focus on the Family featured Lori in its April 1998 and September 2002 editions of Heartlink, a web-based outreach to women's resource/pregnancy centers. In 2009, Lori received her Certificate of Ordination from Victory Christian Center of Austin, and later became a graduate of Victory Christian Bible Institute. In 2011, Lori was awarded the Texas Business Woman of the Year Award given by the Women's Chamber of Commerce of Texas.

Lori still serves as Executive Director of the Austin Pregnancy Resource Center, in addition to these roles:

- Member, National Leadership Alliance of Pregnancy Care Services.
- Advisory board member, Life International, Life International University, Grand Rapids, Mich.
- Member, National College Ministry Task Force for Care Net, Lansdowne, Va.
- She is a past president and Public Relations for Legacy Chair for the Republican Women in Williamson County, Texas.
- Past Mentor for Judge Edna Staudt Teen Mentoring Program with Williamson County
- National consultant, Ethics and Religious Liberties Commission Psalm 139 Project, Nashville, Tenn.
- Founder and Coordinator, Austin Area Life Affirming Coalition, (AALAC) in Central Texas.
- Field representative, Living Alternatives adoption agency, Tyler, Texas.
- Member, University of Texas Campus Ministers, Austin.
- Board member and advisory board member for numerous Pregnancy Resource Centers.
- Board member, Central Texas Coalition for Life.
- Board member, Embrace Initiative
- Member, Austin Area Youth Coalition, Austin Youth for LIFE.
- Member, National Day of Prayer Task Force Committee.
- Secretary of the Board, Servants to the City in Austin.
- Past Board Member, Austin Bridge Builders Alliance (ABBA)
- Non-profit Council Member (ABBA)
- Regional Consultant, Zurvita Corporation
- Partner and Austin Ambassador, Loving Shepherd Ministries (international).
- Featured speaker for Ambassador Speakers Bureau
- Host of her own radio show entitled: "It's a New Day!" on *The Bridge* 1120 am

- 2016 Recipient of the North Dallas Professional Women Community Service Award
- Zig Ziglar Legacy Certified Trainer

Lori resides in Round Rock, Texas, where there really is a round rock! She enjoys spending time with her beloved niece from Indiana and her dog Ariel, Ari for short.

To contact Lori DeVillez call 512-971-7999 or email Lori at ldevillez@gmail.com.